Eyewitness
SHARK
Expert Files

Eyewitness
SHARK
Expert Files

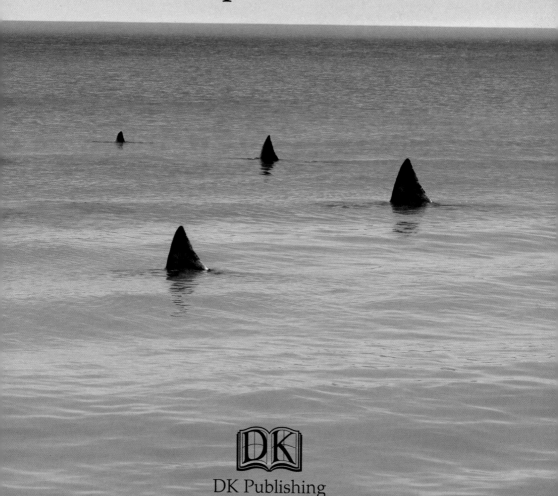

DK Publishing

LONDON, NEW YORK,
MELBOURNE, MUNICH, and DELHI

Consultant Frances Dipper
Senior Editor Jayne Miller
Editors Jaqueline Fortey, Lisa Stock
Senior Art Editor Edward Kinsey
Art Editors Chloe Luxford, Susan
St. Louis, Gemma Thompson
Paper Engineer Chloe Luxford
Managing Editor Camilla Hallinan
Art Director Martin Wilson
Picture Research Harriet Mills
DK Picture Library Claire Bowers
Production Editor Andy Hilliard
Senior Production Controller Man Fai Lau
Jacket Designer Dave Ball
Eyewitness Experts concept Caroline Buckingham

First published in the United States in 2008
by DK Publishing,
375 Hudson Street, New York, New York 10014

08 09 10 11 10 9 8 7 6 5 4 3 2 1
ED625– 07/08

A catalog record for this book
is available from the Library of Congress.

ISBN: 978–0–7566–4018–7

Color reproduction by Colourscan, Singapore
Printed and bound by Toppan Printing Co.
(Shenzhen) Ltd., China

Discover more at
www.dk.com

Contents

1

MEET THE EXPERTS

What's it like to swim with the largest sharks in the world? Meet a shark expert who's dived into the deep to discover more about the lives of some of the most fascinating creatures on the planet.

marine biologist

EXPERT PROFILE

Rachel Graham

NAME: **RACHEL GRAHAM**

LOCATION: **BELIZE**

LIVES: **BELIZE & US**

Rachel Graham studied zoology (a branch of science investigating animals) at Oxford University in the UK. She has always been fascinated by the sea and learned how to dive in 1986. Rachel's work means that she is rarely at home and has lived most of her life abroad working on environmental projects in Egypt, Africa, the United States, South America, Central America, and Britain. She especially enjoyed marine research, so in 1998 she went back to doing field work in Belize. Here she met the whale sharks that have changed the course of her career and her life. Rachel loves her work with whale sharks and other "toothy" sharks, since it involves researching and working on the conservation of top marine predators.

GLADDEN SPIT
The Silk Cayes, where Rachel's camp was based, are located south of Gladden Spit, an elbow-shaped stretch of reef jutting into the water near the Belize Barrier Reef. The area became a protected marine reserve in May 2000.

The wonders of whale sharks

BELIZE ON THE MAP
The Silk Cayes (pronounced keys, like quays) are part of the 185-mile (297-km) barrier reef that fringes Belize. This small country is on the east coast of Central America, just below Mexico. It has a subtropical climate.

WHEN OUR EXPERT CAME FACE TO FACE WITH THE LARGEST SHARKS ON THE PLANET, SHE WONDERED WHY THESE HUGE WHALE SHARKS GATHERED IN BELIZE. SINCE THEN SHE HAS DEDICATED YEARS TO THEIR RESEARCH AND TO THEIR PROTECTION.

GENTLE GIANT
Whale sharks are the largest of all living sharks. They are also filter feeders, not hunters, so researchers can get up close to find out more about their habits and lifestyle. Here Rachel's assistants Julie Berry and Nia Cherrett swim with one of the locals.

Dog snappers spawning in Belize

LIFE IN THE DEEP
Snapper fish are drawn to Belize from far away to reproduce at a specific time in the lunar cycle—and attract many larger fish and sharks.

Big surprise

Initially, I hadn't gone to Belize to study whale sharks. I had decided to go back to field work in marine biology and in 1998 I joined colleagues in Belize who wanted a zoologist and dive master to work with them on a project investigating reef fish and spawning aggregations. This is where many reef fish come together at a particular time and place to reproduce. It was spectacular to see—thousands and thousands of big fish coming together and reproducing at dusk. What's more, huge whale sharks were gathering to feed on the eggs that the fish were releasing. I couldn't believe how big the sharks were when they first appeared through a curtain of fish. Yet they were so graceful. They swam inches away and turned gently around to inspect us in the water.

An evening dip

We had no idea that this area in Belize was the only place in the world where you can see this happening predictably. Nobody did. The local fishermen just said, "Fish come together to spawn here. Oh, and there are some big sharks, too." There were *lots* of big sharks. The fishermen knew they were whale sharks—in Belize they are called Sapodilla Tom—but no one realized they were appearing like clockwork in the late afternoon at certain times of the year and always at a particular spot. By diving with the sharks at dusk we could get

"The whale shark is the diamond in the diver's crown—it's top of the list of what they want to see"

Whale sharks coming to feed

Local fishermen, local knowledge

had not been published. I formulated questions that could be tested scientifically and would form the basis of my research. Do whale sharks live at Gladden Spit all the time? If not, where do they live when they are not feeding? Do the same sharks come back each year and if so, how many? I was determined to plot the movement of whale sharks—but how? You can't follow them because the seas are often very rough and they do not always swim at the surface.

to see this marine marvel first hand. Since then, there has been a big increase in diving and also in the awareness of what a whale shark is. Now, the whale shark is the diamond in the diver's crown—it's top of the list of what they want to see, then a reef shark and then a great white—but at that time, no one was interested in whale sharks. There was so much I wanted to know about them. Are they attracted just to those fish spawning at Gladden Spit, and snappers especially, or are they attracted to a range of spawning fish?

Change of direction

From then on, my colleagues focused on the oceanographic features of the area and the spawning, and I focused on the whale sharks. We set up base on the desert island closest to the Belize barrier reef. On that first trip in 1998, we stayed for just two weeks, camping on the island and investigating the fish and sharks. It took a couple of trips to work out what to do and to plan the research. Back on dry land, I looked up what was known about whale sharks and found that there was little biological or behavioral information on this species. Some research had been conducted in Australia, and some tagging in Mexico, but most of the work

Planning a proposal

I needed to find the tools and funding that would help me answer these questions. I realized that this was a big project, so I might as well do the research as part of a PhD, my next educational qualification. Having worked out a proposal and a budget, I found an adviser, Callum Roberts at York University, who took me on as his student. One of the things we were looking at was how to turn the spawning site into a protected area. Luckily, I managed to get funding from two government bodies in the UK that fund research into biodiversity, or protecting species.

FIRST THE FISH
Researchers regularly measure and weigh samples to gauge the health of the fish at Gladden Spit. The whale sharks only come to Gladden because of the fish.

Setting up camp

We are talking about an island no bigger than a football field. A tucked-away desert island with palm trees, and nothing else. There was no water, no facilities. We had to bring in everything: boat gas, SCUBA tanks, food and shelter, and all the rest of our equipment. We had some tremendous storms that blew down our tents and had us chasing after our equipment in the middle of the night.

Sunset over Silk Cayes and the campsite

Back with a plan

Eventually I had funding, equipment, and a team, so I could get the project going and start answering all those questions. This meant staying on the island camp for two weeks each month, four months a year, for four years. There are three Cayes, little desert islands behind the barrier reef, and we were on the middle one. Literally in the middle of nowhere!

Teamwork

The team varied from month to month and year to year. Sometimes we had up to 16 people, but there was always a core of eight. When I first started, I had three researchers—an oceanographer, another marine biologist, and me. We also had a cook, and the rest were Belizean fishermen we hired to work with us because they knew the site. The water on each side of the spit has strong

DAILY LIFE

Water for washing, cooking, and drinking had to be brought by boat to the island, along with all provisions. There were no buildings or facilities at all.

Cooking in a makeshift kitchen tent

Tagged whale shark with unique spots

TAGGING
This whale shark is towing a satellite tag that provides Rachel's team with its location whenever it's on the surface.

currents and can be treacherous. We had to go beyond the island and the barrier reef to the research site, Gladden Spit, where the fish came together and the whale sharks came in to feed. Here the reef has a short sloping shelf that drops down steeply to 1½ miles (2 km) in depth. Gladden Spit has since become a protected marine reserve, so no one can camp on Silk Cayes any more. In later trips, we lived on nearby islands and on a catamaran parked behind the barrier reef.

Daily routine

We dived two or three times a day—once in the morning, and once or twice in the afternoon. The most important dive took place at dusk, when I could take photographs, tag sharks, and look out for previously tagged sharks. We used a variety of tags, including numbered marker tags, satellite tags, and acoustic tags, designed to be harmless and to cause little discomfort to the sharks. Acoustic transmitting tags emit a string of pulses

UNDERWATER CAMERAMAN
Most members of the team could do a couple of tasks, including taking pictures or acting as dive masters.

that gives each tag a code. This means a receiver finding a shark with an acoustic tag will capture its distinctive set of pings, so we can identify that particular shark. Marker tags helped us to count and identify visiting sharks quickly. We measured many of them when we tagged them and took photos of individuals for long-term identification. I have thousands of ID photographs of whale sharks. Every whale shark has a unique spot pattern and nicks and scars, so they are easily recognizable. We got to know some of them well over the years. They are gentle and nice to be around, unlike some of the predatory sharks that I've met!

"I have thousands of ID photographs of whale sharks ... every one unique"

Building a picture

Acoustic tags were vital to our discovery that whale sharks increasingly gathered at spawning sites as the day wore on, until there was a peak close to dusk. As soon as spawning was finished, the number of sharks fell. Over the years we were able to build a picture of how they used the site by day and night. The tags also let us know that the same sharks were coming back each year, between March and June. Outside of those months we knew not to waste time there because the whale sharks were scarce and had moved elsewhere. By tracking individual whale sharks' movements we now know that they travel hundreds of miles up the Belize Barrier Reef and beyond to Honduras and Mexico searching for food, but they return to Gladden Spit for the spawning of the snappers.

Playing tag

We also had great success with satellite tags. These are attached to the sharks and stay on them for up to a year gathering information about their diving and temperature preferences as well as movements between where the tags are put on and where they pop off. At a preset date, satellite tags detach from the animals, float up to the surface, and transmit their data to me via a satellite. With sat tags we could see the sharks were diving to depths of at least 5,000 ft (1,500 m), possibly to regulate their temperature, to search for food, or just to take a

Logging data in an island office

"The big critters of the ocean are the most vulnerable to fishing and pollution ... sharks need our protection"

GATHERING CLUES
A researcher swims with a plankton net, used to collect samples of the whale sharks' food when they are not feeding exclusively on spawn.

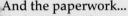

nap. Two of our satellite tags did not detach from the animals as planned. In 2002, we spotted a shark with an old satellite tag on its side. My husband, a Belizean fisherman and a very fast swimmer, swam after the shark and clipped off the tag. It turned out to be chock-full of data on what that shark had been doing minute by minute for 206 days. That one satellite tag was an absolute treasure trove.

And the paperwork...

I had accumulated masses of data, but I made the crucial mistake of not writing it up as I went along! People say you should spend a quarter of your time in the field, and use the rest to analyze and write up data. However, I was spending half of my time in the water and the other half inputting data and preparing for the field trips. Finally, in 2003, I spent a year analyzing the data and writing my thesis. By then, I was expecting a baby so I had to get the reports and the PhD finished before I gave birth. I got it all submitted 36 hours before the baby was born!

A natural solution

Our research helped to make the area a marine reserve in 2000, but there was still strong fishing pressure on the spawning fish, so we looked for economic alternatives for Gladden's fishermen. Tourism was a preferred alternative and so we developed the first whale shark tourism course and helped to sponsor the first dive training for fishermen in Belize. Now over 60 former fishermen guide tourists to the whale shark feeding area each year.

Saving our sharks

My work at Gladden is still ongoing, but on a smaller scale. The local organization Friends of Nature took over the monitoring of the whale sharks and the spawning aggregation. I also work with other shark species, looking at the impact of fishing and helping to promote their conservation. The big critters of the ocean are the most vulnerable to fishing, pollution, and habitat destruction because they generally live a long time, mature late, and have very few young. They are important because they keep the oceans healthy by balancing the populations of many prey species. For this and many other reasons, sharks need our protection.

Listening for acoustically tagged sharks

Types of expert

THE STUDY OF MARINE LIFE includes many fields of expertise. Sometimes scientists work in the laboratory or aquarium doing detailed research on animals and plants. However, going underwater to visit ocean habitats and encounter sharks in the wild is invaluable. Marine fieldwork can involve diving on coral reefs, working as part of a research ship team, or exploring the deep sea in submersibles.

PACIFIC CORAL REEFS
Divers cruise through soft corals on underwater scooters in Palau, Micronesia, a well-known habitat for many tropical shark species.

MARINE BIOLOGIST

The study of life in the oceans, from microscopic plankton to giant whale sharks, is called marine biology. A marine biologist may work for a research institute or university, for a government fishery department that monitors and manages a country's fish stocks, or for a conservation organization run by a charity. It is a career that demands good scientific skills and an interest in the environment. Some specialists focus on a particular animal group, while others do research into life in ocean environments, such as coral reefs or mangrove swamps. As concern grows about the impact of overfishing and pollution on the numbers of sharks and other species, marine biologists play a vital role in maintaining our planet's health and biodiversity.

OCEANOGRAPHER

Scientists who investigate how the oceans work and how they interact with the land, freshwater systems, atmosphere, and ice caps are called oceanographers. They study different aspects, from physical measurements of waves and currents to the chemical composition of seawater and the geology of the seafloor. This is important for understanding the relationship between sharks and their environment.

DIVING IN A SUBMERSIBLE
A mini-sub provides scientists with a window onto a mysterious underwater world.

WALKING THROUGH WATER
Visitors view sharks from below, in Seaworld's huge **Shark Encounter** *Aquarium in Orlando, Florida, USA.*

AQUARIUM RESEARCHER

Many of the world's great aquariums are also marine laboratories and important centres of research. Some scientists work on the best designs to exhibit and care for the animals, based on their natural habitats. Others run captive breeding programmes for bony fish and sharks. More fish bred in captivity means fewer need to be collected from the wild for research and exhibits. Aquariums also provide opportunities for marine biologists to study the behaviour of sharks and other fish. This type of work can be difficult to do in the wild.

ECOTOUR LEADER

Expert divers and naturalist[s] offer boat trips and dives to [w]known habitats, guiding tour[s] places where sharks can be se[en] their natural surroundings. An ecotour leader may use bait t[o] attract the sharks so that the[y] be photographed as they fe[ed]. Swimming alongside whale sharks is also popular. An ec[o] leader has to ensure that tour[ists] are kept safe and avoid disrupt[ing] the sharks' normal activit[ies]

TEMPTING SHARK

A diver lures shark with bait. Great care [must be] taken when feeding sharks. Some scientis[ts] it makes sharks associate humans with fo[od]

FILMMAKERS

An underwater filmmaker or photographer needs to have a passion for marine life and be a confident diver, able to remain steady in the water while taking a good shot. Natural history photography has played a vital role in making people aware of the wonders of life in the oceans. Pioneers in the field often designed their own camera and diving equipment, and skilled technicians are still valued members of teams making documentary films and fictional underwater movies.

DIVING CAGE

A photographer is suspended i[n] water in a strong, metal cage. T[his] brings him face to face with a c[lose] great white shark and gives hi[m] ideal photo opportunity.

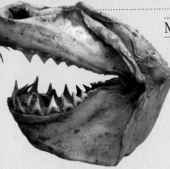

MARINE TAXONOMIST

A marine taxonomist works in a laboratory, aquarium, or natural history museum, naming and classifying ocean animals and plants. This detailed work is vital for identifying previously unknown species. The taxonomist looks at a shark's anatomy to determine what it is and which shark group it belongs to. If it is an example of a new species, it will be given its own scientific name.

JAWS
A shark's skull provides clues to its identity. These are the powerful teeth and jaws of a great white shark.

CONSERVATIONIST

Sharks are hunted for their meat, skin, and liver oil and for their fins, used to make shark fin soup. Shark-finning is a wasteful and rapidly increasing practice that is threatening some species with extinction. Shark conservationists work for campaigns and organizations dedicated to protecting sharks. They include environmental scientists, who monitor shark and ray populations and their habitats. Conservation groups aim to persuade governments and companies to reduce pollution and manage fishing effectively. They also keep the public informed about marine issues.

ADOPT A WHALE SHARK
Conservation organizations raise money to support their campaigns through programs such as "adopting" a shark.

ELECTRONIC TAGS
Experts and volunteers monitor basking sharks in the Irish Sea. This tracker downloads data from shark tags onto a computer.

SHARK TRACKER

To find out more about a shark's home range and migration, scientists and fishermen attach tags to its dorsal fins. The sharks are often given names, such as Tracy or Rolf. Some tags contain a tiny pop-up computer, which stores information. The tag later releases itself and is picked up by a tracker or relays data back to a laboratory by satellite.

Tools and techniques

SHARK EXPERTS WORKING UNDERWATER face many challenges, but they have excellent equipment to help them. New types of dive suits, breathing apparatus, cameras, submersible craft, and protective devices enable divers and photographers to explore the marine world safely. Techniques used with sharks range from state-of-the-art satellite tracking to the traditional fisherman's practice of "chumming."

DIVING EQUIPMENT

The latest breathing equipment enables divers to stay under water for longer and to approach sharks without a tell-tale trail of bubbles. The diver breathes through a mouthpiece linked to a rebreather on his back. This contains cylinders of compressed air and oxygen, and a scrubbing unit to recycle the diver's breath. The diver is also wearing a drysuit, hood, gloves, and mask.

Pure oxygen cylinder

Data link cable to a wrist computer

MOUTHPIECE
The diver breathes in clean air through the mouthpiece. The toxic carbon dioxide in the exhaled gas is removed by the scrubbing unit.

Wrist dive computer

COMPUTER DISPLAY
A computer screen on a monitor strapped to the wrist tells the diver that the oxygen level in the air supply is safe for breathing.

ROBOTIC SHARK
*One way to to get close to sharks is by blending in. Oceanographer Fabian Cousteau was inspired by a famous **Tintin** story to design a submarine that looks just like a great white shark.*

Sub measures 14 ft (4 m) from tail to tip of nose

Diver enters access and escape hatch

EXPLORATION

Diving and trips in submersibles allow researchers to explore the underwater world. Ideally, they need to see sharks behaving as naturally as possible. Vibrating engines and bubbles released by scuba diving equipment can alert sharks to the approach of spectators. Fabian Cousteau's robotic shark sub moves silently and looks just like a great white, so it can move and film undetected among the sharks. The sub operator tries to move and behave naturally to avoid attack. He can report observations through wireless contact with the support ship above.

INSIDE THE SUB
The water-filled 14-ft (4-m) shark sub has steel ribs, an elastic skin, and a motor. Cameras give the diver-operator a view of what is happening all around.

Steel supports

Diver operates water-filled sub

CHUMMING AND BAITING

A man-made scent trail that attracts fish is called chum. Ecotour operators use it to attract sharks to places where they can be photographed and filmed. A smelly mixture made of ground-up small fish, such as herring and pilchards, is placed in a container with holes. This is suspended from a boat on a line, releasing an oily film onto the water surface. Researchers may use larger carcasses as bait. Some states in the US require a permit for chumming and baiting sharks.

BAITED LINE
This great white shark was photographed by top underwater photographer Valerie Taylor, as it lunged at bait dragged on a line from a boat.

Hall of fame

OVER THE YEARS, MANY PEOPLE have made a profound contribution to our knowledge of sharks and their behavior. These include scientists, conservationists, and writers, as well as divers and filmmakers, who have given these amazing creatures popular appeal.

ARISTOTLE
384–322 BCE
JOB: Natural philosopher
COUNTRY: Ancient Greece

Aristotle was the first person in the Western world to investigate living things and classify them into groups. He dissected sharks and other animal species in order to describe their anatomy. His research was published in his work *Historia Animalium* in 350 BCE.

WILLIAM BEEBE
1877–1962
JOB: Naturalist/diver/writer
COUNTRY: US

In the early 20th century few people had seen ocean animals in their natural habitat. Naturalist Dr. Charles William Beebe designed his

William Beebe

own hard helmet to make dives in shallow water in the 1930s and made first-hand observations of shark behavior. He joined forces with explorer and inventor Otis Barton to develop a diving vehicle for deeper water—the bathysphere. It was a cast iron and steel sphere with portholes, a spotlight, supplies of electricity and oxygen, and a cable and telephone link to the mother ship. In August 1934, the intrepid divers were lowered in the bathysphere to a depth of 3,028 ft (923 m) beneath the ocean. Beebe's books and articles inspired a new generation of undersea explorers.

PETER BENCHLEY
1940–2006
JOB: Writer/broadcaster
COUNTRY: US

The story of *Jaws*, the great white shark that terrorized people in a beach resort, thrilled readers and filmgoers across the globe. Peter Benchley, author of the novel and screenplay for the blockbuster film, was propelled to international fame by its success. Benchley owed his fascination with sharks to family fishing trips. He was working as a journalist in 1964 when an enormous great white shark was caught off Long Island and the idea for *Jaws* was born. The 1974 novel was followed by other books, articles, television, and radio shows. Benchley later regretted the shark's negative image and became a conservation campaigner and a member of the US National Council of Environmental Defense.

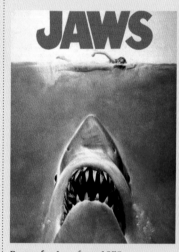

Poster for *Jaws* from 1975

GEORGE H. BURGESS
1949 TO PRESENT
JOB: Ichthyologist
COUNTRY: US

The Florida Museum of Natural History is a leading center for shark research, with an excellent website. The museum's coordinator of operations is George H. Burgess, an ichthyologist—an expert on sharks and other fishes—specializing in the southeastern United States, the Gulf of Mexico, and the Caribbean. His photos of sharks illustrate many books and articles. He is curator of the International Shark Attack File, which monitors the interactions between humans and sharks. As vice chairman of the World Conservation Union's Shark Specialist Group, he is part of a team of experts dedicated to protecting shark species.

DR. EUGENIE CLARK

1922 TO PRESENT

JOB: Ichthyologist/writer

COUNTRY: US

Eugenie Clark's love for fish began when she visited an aquarium as a child in New York. Nicknamed "The Shark Lady," she is renowned for her studies of shark behavior, and for her writing, films, and teaching. She has received over 25 medals and awards, including a Women of Discovery Award in 2006. During her career she has made over 71 submersible dives, captured and studied over 2,000 sharks, and worked on developing shark repellants. She was a founder of the Center for Shark Research, at Mote Marine Laboratory, Florida.

LEONARD J. V. COMPAGNO

1943 TO PRESENT

JOB: Ichthyologist

COUNTRY: US/SOUTH AFRICA

Dr. Leonard Compagno is the world's leading expert on shark taxonomy. He is the director of the Shark Research center at the Iziko South African Museum, Cape Town, the hub of international shark studies. The shark biologist's "bible" is a two-volume catalog of shark species compiled by Compagno for FAO (the UN Food and Agriculture Organization). He is also author, with Sarah Fowler, of the definitive *Collins Field Guide to the Sharks of the World,* which covers all 530 known species.

JACQUES COUSTEAU

1910–1997

JOB: Filmmaker and writer

COUNTRY: France

Pioneer diver and world-famous filmmaker, Jacques Cousteau brought the wonderful world of sharks and other marine life to people's TV screens for the first time. In 1943 with Emile Gagnan, he invented the aqualung, an underwater breathing apparatus that enabled divers to move freely underwater. Aboard his ship *Calypso*, a converted mine-sweeper, he developed underwater film techniques and made at least 100 documentaries. Experts from a wide variety of fields joined him on his voyages. He was an active environmental campaigner, successfully fighting in the 1960s against the dumping of radioactive waste in the Mediterranean Sea.

Jacques
Cousteau

SYLVIA EARLE

1935 TO PRESENT

JOB: Marine biologist/writer

COUNTRY: US

Sylvia Earle began her career as a specialist in marine plants and has become a living legend in undersea research. In 1969 she was part of an all-female team on *Tectite II*, an underwater research station, where divers lived for long periods under water. For many years she has been at the cutting edge of exploration and diving technology, including the design of deepsea submersibles. She has worked as a government chief scientist and adviser, and is a keen conservationist, highlighting the sharp decline in the numbers of sharks and other predatory fish.

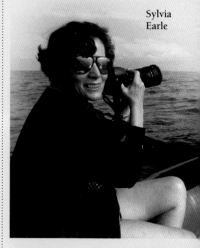

Sylvia
Earle

SARAH FOWLER OBE

1958 TO PRESENT

JOB: Environmental consultant

COUNTRY: UK

Zoologist Sarah Fowler received an OBE for her contribution to marine conservation in 2004. She has played a key role in campaigns to protect sharks and rays. She is currently Managing Director of Nature Bureau International, an environmental consultancy based in the UK. She is also cofounder of the European Elasmobranch Association and the UK Shark Trust, which organizes campaigns on shark conservation and shark fishery management. The Shark Trust website contains activities and facts sheets for children.

RODNEY FOX

DATE: 1940 TO PRESENT

JOB: Filmmaker and conservationist

COUNTRY: Australia

In 1963, Rodney Fox survived one of the worst known attacks by a great white shark. Despite this terrifying encounter, he has spent over 40 years studying sharks and campaigning to protect them. He has designed diving cages to enable researchers to get closer to white sharks and runs boat trips to watch them in the wild. His Shark Museum in Adelaide, South Australia, houses displays of his filmmaking expeditions and a great collection of shark teeth.

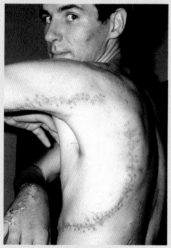

Fox pictured soon after the attack

AL GIDDINGS

1937 TO PRESENT

JOB: Filmmaker/producer

COUNTRY: US

Al Giddings is an award-winning underwater filmmaker and camera systems engineer who has worked as director, producer, and cinematographer on at least 50 documentary films and blockbuster movies, including *Shark Chronicles* for IMAX, which won an award for cinematography, and *Live from a Shark Cage, The Deep, Titanic,* and *The Abyss*. He was the first to film the great white shark in slow motion. Responding to the technical challenges of filming underwater, he designed a motorized cage for filming, special camera and lighting systems, and created film sets in huge tanks of water. Giddings has worked with leading researchers worldwide, including Sylvia Earle, and filmed in every major ocean, spending a total of 20,000 hours under water—so far. Giddings is also involved in underwater photography for high-definition TV.

SAMUEL GRUBER

1938 TO PRESENT

JOB: Ichthyologist

COUNTRY: US

In the tropical waters around Bimini Biological Field Station in the Bahamas, Samuel "Doc" Gruber and his graduate students study lemon sharks. The Bimini team have done exceptional work on their courtship behavior. Dr. Gruber, the station's founder and director, owes his choice of career to a close encounter with a hammerhead on a spearfishing trip as a teenager. He has led 49 research expeditions in the Atlantic and is a world authority on many aspects of shark biology, behavior, and ecology. As the founder of the World Conservation Union Shark Specialist Group, he is at the forefront of shark conservation.

Dr. Sam Gruber

HANS HASS

1919 TO PRESENT

JOB: Diver/documentary maker

COUNTRY: Austria

In the 1930s and 1940s, Hans Hass pioneered underwater photography and became a shark enthusiast. He took his first photograph under water in 1938, and soon gave up studying law to become a zoologist. In the 1940s, Hass started to "swimdive," with lighter-weight breathing apparatus and flippers to give himself greater freedom of movement. Using this equipment, he risked his life alone in the Red Sea to film *Men among Sharks* in 1947. He made many documentary films with his wife Lotte.

HERODOTUS

CA. 484–425 BCE

JOB: Historian

COUNTRY: Ancient Greece

Herodotus of Halicarnassus was the first historian and author of *The Histories*, which were a mixture of fact and folklore. They give an account of a storm off the Mount Athos peninsula on the northern coast of Greece in 492 BCE that wrecked an invading Persian army. Many of the shipwrecked mariners were attacked and killed by "sea monsters" in the Aegean Sea. This is the earliest known account of shark attacks at sea.

Bust of Herodotus

GUILLAUME RONDELET
1507–1566
JOB: Naturalist and physician
COUNTRY: France

This 16th-century Professor of Medicine from the University of Montpellier kept fish in tanks at his suburban villa and wrote the first natural history of fishes, illustrated with woodcuts. Rondelet described a huge fish with a voracious appetite, which is likely to have been a great white shark. His book remained an important work until Swedish taxonomists Peter Artedi and Carl Linnaeus began to name and classify fish, including sharks, in the 18th century.

STEWART SPRINGER
1906–1991
JOB: Ichthyologist
COUNTRY: US

Stewart Springer dropped out of university when he was young, but this did not prevent him from

becoming a world expert on sharks. He was a highly skilled field biologist, fascinated by shark behavior. Over 35 species of sharks and rays were classified or named by him, and he was a cofounder of the Shark Attack File. He was employed as a fishery biologist by the US Fish and Wildlife Service, where he ran shark tagging programs.

Tooth fossil

JEREMY STAFFORD-DEITSCH
1958 TO PRESENT
JOB: Marine photographer
COUNTRY: UK

Snorkeling in the Mediterranean inspired Jeremy Stafford-Deitsch's career choice. He became an acclaimed professional marine photographer, with a special interest in sharks. His first field trip was to Sam Gruber's famous Bimini Field Station in the Bahamas. His magnificent pictures appear in many books, including *Shark—A Photographer's Story* and *Red Sea Sharks*. He prefers to work alone, capturing images of sharks in their particular habitats, using naturalistic lighting. He is also a patron of the UK-based Shark Trust.

Valerie Taylor in a chain-mail diving suit

NIELS STENSEN
1638–1686
JOB: Anatomist and geologist
COUNTRY: Denmark

Also known as Nicholas Steno, Stensen was the first to identify fossil sharks' teeth. In 1666, he dissected the head of a Mediterranean great white shark. He compared its teeth with "tongue stones," which people believed fell from the sky, and showed that they derived from the teeth of ancient sharks.

VALERIE TAYLOR
1936 TO PRESENT
JOB: Photographer/shark expert
COUNTRY: Australia

Award-winning photographer and shark expert Valerie Taylor met her husband Ron at a spearfishing championship. Their early interest in fishing turned into a passion for conservation. They have spent 50 years making underwater documentary films and pioneered the use of chain mail to protect divers from shark bites. Valerie won the American Photographer of the Year Award in 1997 and in 2000 was honored in the American Women Divers Hall of Fame.

② ACTIVITIES

Have you got what it takes to be a marine biologist? Find out how much you know and sharpen your shark skills with our challenging activities.

Which expert are you?

Inspired by the work of our experts, you must have decided that a career involving sharks is for you. The problem is that it all sounds so exciting, so how do you choose what area to go into? Try our fun flowchart and find out.

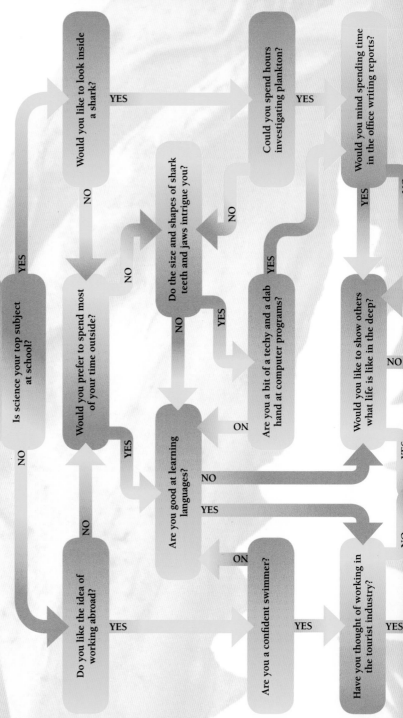

START HERE

Is science your top subject at school?

Would you like to look inside a shark?

YES

Could you spend hours investigating plankton?

YES

Would you mind spending time in the office writing reports?

YES

Do the size and shapes of shark teeth and jaws intrigue you?

Would you prefer to spend most of your time outside?

YES

NO

NO

NO

YES

YES

Are you a bit of a techy and a dab hand at computer programs?

YES

ON

Would you like to show others what life is like in the deep?

NO

Are you good at learning languages?

NO

YES

ON

YES

Do you like the idea of working abroad?

NO

YES

Are you a confident swimmer?

ON

YES

Have you thought of working in the tourist industry?

YES

ON

Do you want to learn about sharks' habits and life cycle?

YES →

Would you like to care for sharks close up?

NO →

Would you stay calm with sharks swimming around you?

NO →

Do you worry whether it's wrong to breed sharks in captivity?

NO →

YES →

Could you cope with coachloads of kids asking you questions?

NO

YES

Could you put the safety of others first?

YES

NO →

Are you often taking pictures on your cell or camera?

NO

YES →

ECOTOUR LEADER

You would hate to be tied to the office when there is a vast ocean out there to explore. You love traveling, diving, and meeting people. Just don't take any risks!

PHOTOGRAPHER

Your passion for sharks and sea life is matched only by your enjoyment of film. You'd love to dive to the depths, coming back with images of rare, amazing creatures.

AQUARIUM WORKER

Observing sharks and getting to know their habits close-up is a thrill, and being able to share your knowledge to encourage experts of the future would be an ideal mix.

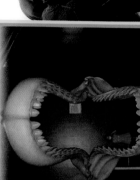

MARINE BIOLOGIST

You would be happy working in the field and following up research at home, alone or as part of a team. You are fascinated with what makes sharks tick and where they spend their lives.

Which am I?

Can you spot the differences between a shark and other types of fish? Read the list of labels for the spinner shark and the bony fish shown below, then write the labels in the correct places. We have done the first two for you.

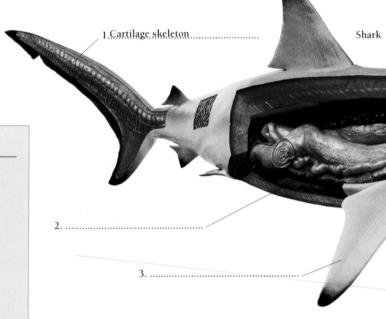

1.Cartilage skeleton......................

Shark

2. ....

3. ....

SHARK LABELS

No cover on gill slits
Rigid fin
Cartilage skeleton
Sandpapery skin
Mouth beneath snout
Oil-filled liver

BONY FISH LABELS

Covered gill slits
Flexible fin
Bony skeleton
Scaly skin
Mouth at end of snout
Gas-filled swim bladder

1. ....

2. ....

3. Bony skeleton...............................

4. ....

Open up *Eyewitness Shark* for some inside knowledge about sharks and bony fish.

Bony fish or shark?

Now label these pictures, choosing between shark and bony fish!

Use your Profile Cards to help you spot the difference.

4. ....

5. ....

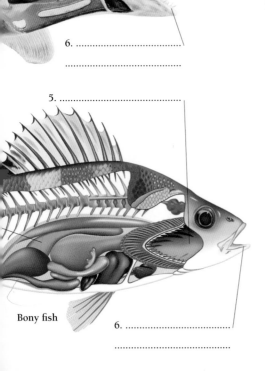

6. ....

....

5. ....

Bony fish

6. ....

....

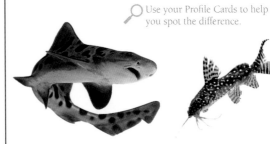

A. ....   B. ....

C. ....

D. ....

E. ....

F. ....

G. ....

What do I eat?

LEVEL 1

A shark's teeth and jaws give clues to the type of food it eats. Can you guess the shark from its eating habits? Choosing from the list of six sharks below, fill in the name of each shark, then match the shark with the prey on the facing page.

HOW LONG
DID IT TAKE YOU?

☐ 10 mins:
Expert

☐ 15 mins:
Knowledgable

☐ 20 mins:
Beginner

NAME THE SHARKS	
Great white	Tiger
Sand tiger	Port Jackson
Basking	Great hammerhead

My teeth are small and my jaws are powerful.

1. ....

I have rows of curved, serrated teeth like chainsaws.

2. ....

My teeth are tiny and not used when I eat.

3. ....

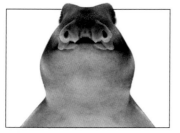

I use my head to hold down fish living on the sea bottom.

4. ....

I have large, wide, triangular teeth for cutting large prey.

5. ....

My narrow, sharp, curved teeth can grasp slippery prey.

6. ....

Shark snacks

To check shark menus, look at your *Eyewitness Shark* and Profile Cards.

Under each picture, fill in the name of the prey and add the number of the shark most likely to eat it.

A. .... ☐

B. .... ☐

C. .... ☐

D. .... ☐

E. .... ☐

F. .... ☐

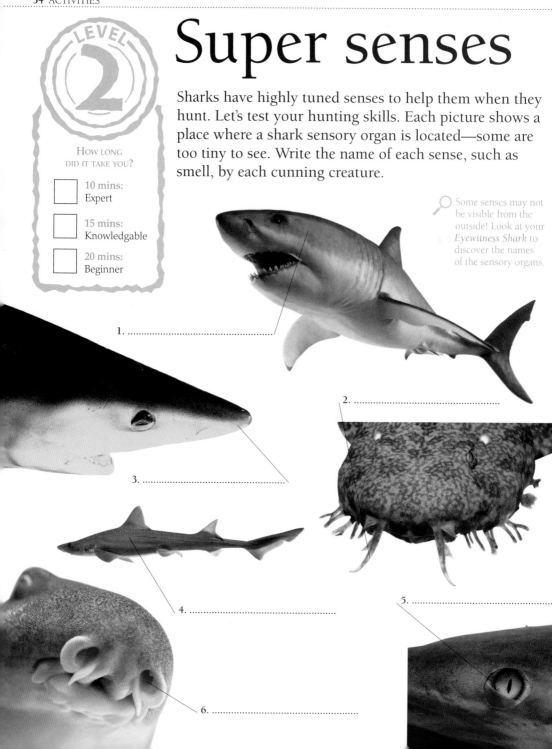

Super senses

Sharks have highly tuned senses to help them when they hunt. Let's test your hunting skills. Each picture shows a place where a shark sensory organ is located—some are too tiny to see. Write the name of each sense, such as smell, by each cunning creature.

HOW LONG
DID IT TAKE YOU?

☐ 10 mins:
Expert

☐ 15 mins:
Knowledgable

☐ 20 mins:
Beginner

Some senses may not be visible from the outside! Look at your *Eyewitness Shark* to discover the names of the sensory organs.

1. ....

2. ....

3. ....

4. ....

5. ....

6. ....

Find the tail

HOW LONG
DID IT TAKE YOU?

☐ 10 mins:
Expert

☐ 15 mins:
Knowledgable

☐ 20 mins:
Beginner

The shape of the tail of a shark or ray can tell you something about how it lives and moves. Match the tail to the description below the pictures and write the correct number in the box. Then fill in the name of each shark.

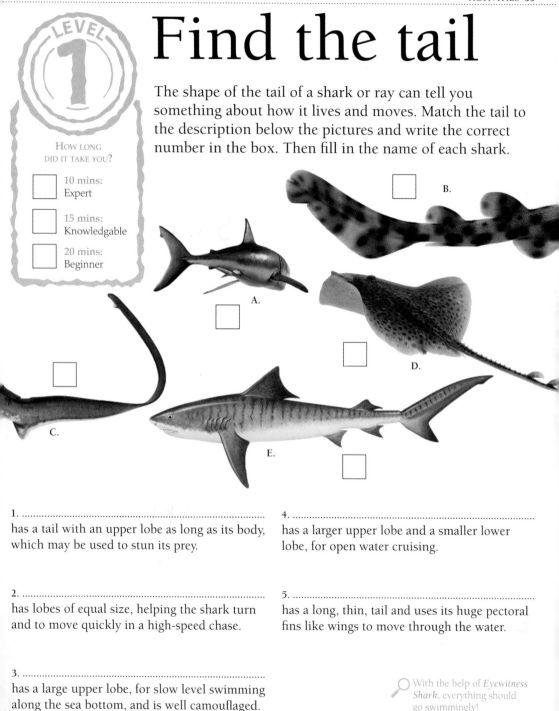

A.

B.

C.

D.

E.

1. ....
has a tail with an upper lobe as long as its body, which may be used to stun its prey.

2. ....
has lobes of equal size, helping the shark turn and to move quickly in a high-speed chase.

3. ....
has a large upper lobe, for slow level swimming along the sea bottom, and is well camouflaged.

4. ....
has a larger upper lobe and a smaller lower lobe, for open water cruising.

5. ....
has a long, thin, tail and uses its huge pectoral fins like wings to move through the water.

With the help of *Eyewitness Shark*, everything should go swimmingly!

Guess who?

Sharks come in so many shapes and sizes that identifying different species can be a challenge. See if you can name each shark from its silhouette. There is a clue to help you! Then write in the size of the shark.

A.

Name

Sall Shark

Size

Clue

My snout is stunning!

B.

Name

Size

Clue

I look a little like an eel.

C.

Name

GalBlin

Size

Clue

I live in deep, dark water.

Name

Leopard

Size

Clue

My stripes change to spots.

D.

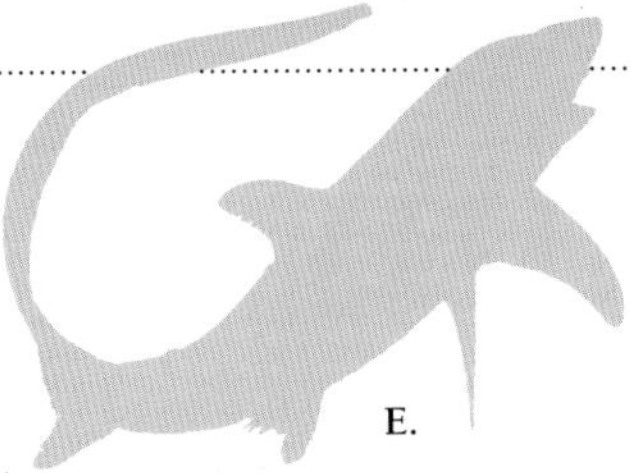

Name

Thresher.

Size

Clue

Watch out for my long tail.

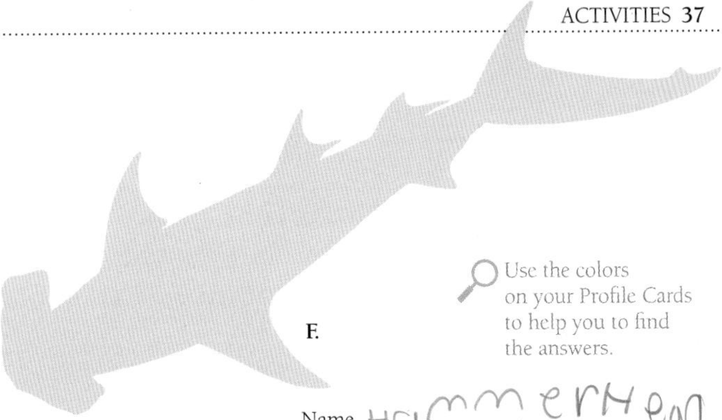

E.

F.

Use the colors
on your Profile Cards
to help you to find
the answers.

Name HaMMerHead.
SmooTh

Size

Clue

Stingrays beware!

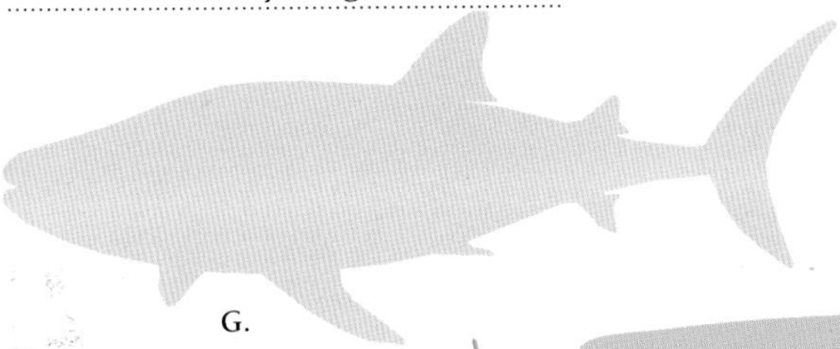

G.

Name

W HaLeShark.

Size

Clue

I am the largest shark.

H.

Name

Size

Clue

I am the smallest shark.

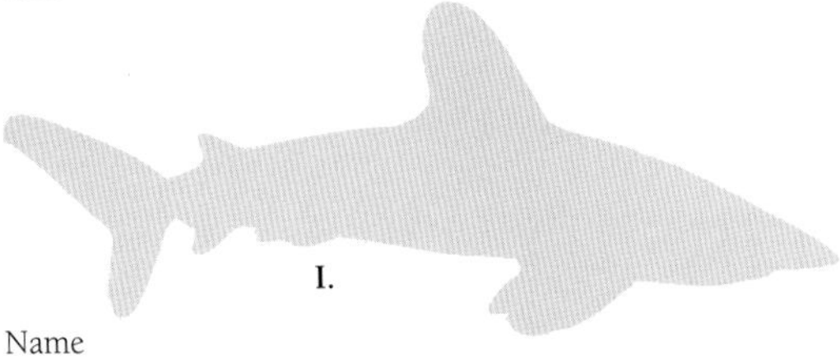

I.

Name

Size

Clue

My fins are tipped with white.

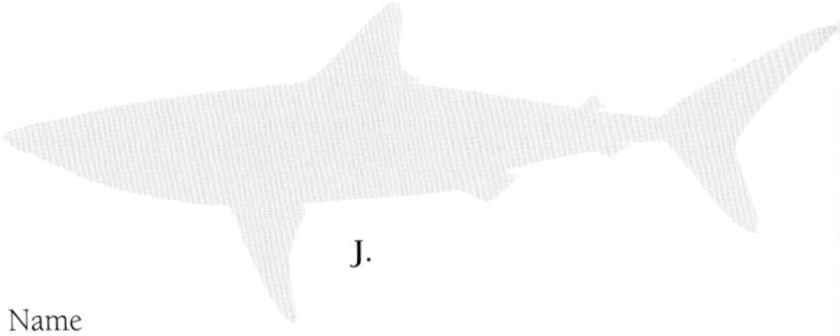

J.

Name

Size

Clue

I am the fastest in the ocean.

Where am I?

Here's your chance to help some sharks discover
where they should be. Can you name the oceans
and point these sharks in the right direction?

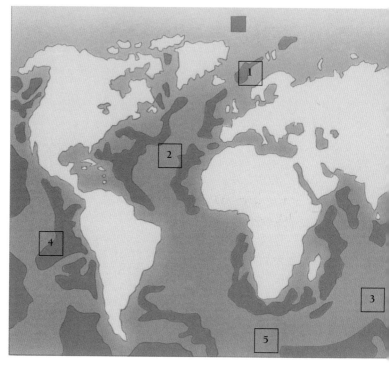

Name the oceans

Some sharks prefer shallow water on the edges
of continents, while others roam the open sea.
See if you can name all the oceans shown.

1. ....

2. ....

3. ....

4. ....

5. ....

Compass

Fill in the points on this
compass rose, working
clockwise from the top
of the picture.

1. ....

8. ....

7. ....

6. ....

2. ....

3. ....

4. ....

5. ....

Place the shark

Fill in the correct name for each shark from the list.
Look out—there is one extra to trick you! Then
write down the map numbers for the oceans where
they are found.

NAME THE SHARK

~~Port Jackson~~
~~Leopard~~
~~Black tip reef~~
~~Nurse~~
Velvet belly lantern
~~Bull~~
~~Basking~~
~~Great white~~
~~Blue~~
Swell

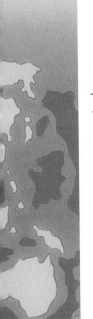

A. Velvet belly lantern.

B. Port Jacksan. C. Leopard.

D. Nurse

E. Bull

F. Great White

G. Black tip reef.

H. Basking

I. Blue.

EXPERTS' LOG

3

It's time to get organized and start your own research. Don't just dive in at the deep end, check out the simple tools and skills that every budding expert needs and find out what you can do to help save sharks.

At the museum

Visiting a natural history museum is a great way to discover more about living sharks, as well as learning about extinct species that hunted millions of years ago

In the field

TOP TIPS

Tools:
• Pen and pencil
• Notebook
• Camera

• Plan a visit to an aquarium where you will see sharks from oceans across the world. Some aquariums have tunnels through glass tanks so you can walk right underneath the water with sharks on either side!

• There is a lot of information to take in. Try to find out as much as you can about your favorite shark. What are its key features? How did it get its name? What does it like to eat? Note down the answers to all your questions here.

• Get involved! Much of the expert knowledge gathered around the world relies on volunteers. If you are by the sea, join a shark watch program, such as Basking Shark Watch, where you record the details of your sightings. Or join an egg case hunt. (See page 63 of *Eyewitness Shark* to learn more.) Keeping precise records is vital!

• If you want a souvenir shark artifact such as a shark tooth, only buy a copy from a museum or aquarium so you won't encourage dealers to kill sharks for their teeth and jaws.

• If you are lucky enough to live in or visit an area with plenty of sharks, you could join an organized snorkeling or boat trip with a reputable instructor.

The best way to learn about sharks is by coming face to face with one! Visit an underwater world at an aquarium for an unforgettable shark encounter.

Research

Books
Books are an essential resource for research. Visit your local library or bookstore to look up a shark you have heard about in the news or have seen in an aquarium, and find out lots of interesting facts about the species.

The media
Keep an eye on the news to find out about rare shark sightings as well as the results of ongoing research projects, such as tagging schemes. Look out for nature programs and documentaries about sharks on television. If you hear about a species that doesn't feature in your Profile Cards, why not make a new card to add to your collection?

The web
Use the internet to find out more about your favorite sharks and the threats they face. Conservation groups such as the World Wide Fund for Nature and the Shark Research Unit have very helpful sites. See the listings on page 69 of *Eyewitness Shark*.

Museums and aquariums
Contact your nearest natural history museum or aquarium to find out if they have an exhibition or event which you would find interesting.

An expert devotes a lot of time to patient research. This is also a great way for you to increase your knowledge and is an important part of your study.

....

....

....

....

....

....

....

....

....

Scrapbook

Use this space to attach your sketches and photographs, and any postcards you have bought. Have a go at drawing a great white, or another fascinating shark you've studied.

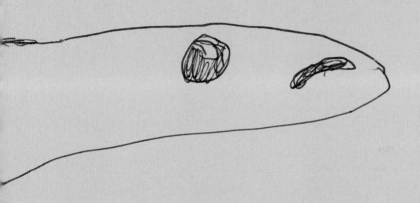

4

PACK MANUAL

Make the most of your interactive expert pack, from creating stunning projects to investigating shark movements on your map. Then follow the step-by-step instructions to make a 3-D model of a great white.

Expert reads

Everything you need to know about getting the most from your interactive expert pack is right here. Written by the experts of today for the experts of tomorrow, these reads will speed you on your journey to uncover the mysteries of the underwater world of sharks. Read on!

Eyewitness Book

This museum in a book is a perfect start to your research. Turn the pages and be an eyewitness to the magnificent sharks of all different shapes and sizes, hidden in the depths of the ocean. Written by experts and illustrated with incredible close-up photographs, *Eyewitness Shark* is an essential read for every budding expert.

Wall chart

When did the first sharks exist? How do sharks breathe under water? Put this chart on your wall at home or at school and the answers to those biting questions will never be far away.

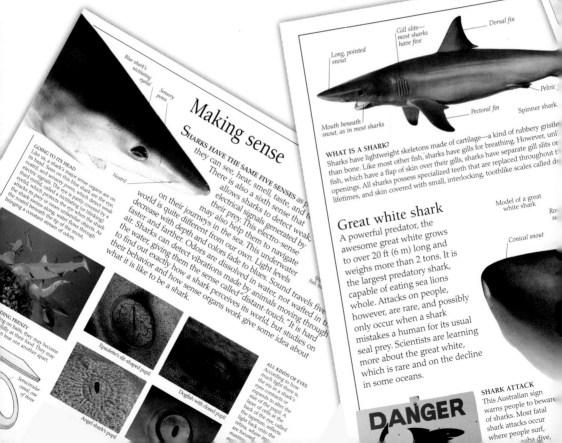

11 PACIFIC ANGE
Squatina californica

PECTORAL FINS
Winglike pectoral fins are broad and flat, and separate from the head.

TAIL
Long tail with large caudal fin aids liftoff from the seabed.

FIELD NOT
Angel sha
the seabe
squashe
rears u
numb

FAC
G

Making sense

SHARKS HAVE THE SAME FIVE SENSES as p
they can see, hear, smell, taste, and h
There is also a sixth sense that
allows sharks to detect weak
electrical signals generated by
their prey. This electro-sense
may also help them to navigate
on their journeys in the sea. This underwater
world is quite different from our own. Light levels
decrease with depth and colors fade to blues. Sound travels five
faster and farther. Odors are dissolved in water, not wafted in th
air. Sharks can detect vibrations made by animals moving through
the water, giving them the sense called "distant-touch." It is hard
to find out exactly how a shark perceives its world, but studies on
their behavior and how sense organs work give some idea about
what it is like to be a shark.

GOING TO ITS HEAD
Like us, a shark's major sense organs are on its head. Seen on this blue shark are the eye, nostril, and sensory pores, which detect weak electric signals. The eye is partly covered by a third eyelid, called a nictitating (or blinking) eyelid, which protects the eye when the shark attacks its prey or nears unfamiliar objects. As the shark swims along, water flows through the nostril beneath the tip of the snout, bringing a constant stream of odors.

Blue shark's nictitating eyelid

Sensory pores

Nostril

DING FRENZY
ng on baits, they may become ndly at the scent of blood. They may n tear one another apart.

Semicircular canal, one of three

Epaulette's slit-shaped pupil

Dogfish with closed pupil

Angel shark's pupil

ALL KINDS OF EYES
According to how much light there is, the iris in a shark's eyes contracts or expands to alter the size of the pupil. A layer of cells at the back of the eye, called the tapetum, reflects light back onto the retina, where im are focused maxim av

What is a shark?

Sharks have lightweight skeletons made of cartilage—a kind of rubbery gristle
than bone. Like most other fish, sharks have gills for breathing. However, unl
fish, which have a flap of skin over their gills, sharks have separate gill slits or
openings. All sharks possess specialized teeth that are replaced throughout t
lifetimes, and skin covered with small, interlocking, toothlike scales called d

Gill slits— most sharks have five

Dorsal fin

Long, pointed snout

Pelvic

Pectoral fin

Spinner shark

Mouth beneath snout, as in most sharks

Great white shark

A powerful predator, the awesome great white grows to over 20 ft (6 m) long and weighs more than 2 tons. It is the largest predatory shark, capable of eating sea lions whole. Attacks on people, however, are rare, and possibly only occur when a shark mistakes a human for its usual seal prey. Scientists are learning more about the great white, which is rare and on the decline in some oceans.

Model of a great white shark

Conical snout

Ro se

SHARK ATTACK
This Australian sign warns people to beware of sharks. Most fatal shark attacks occur where people surf,

DANGER

17 ZEBRA SHARK
Stegostoma fasciatum

FIELD NOTES
This shark is often seen by divers, lying arou[...] reefs. With its long ridged body and spotty [...] to identify, but young sharks have stripes i[...] instead of spots. At night the shark squirm[...] crevices searching for hidden crabs and s[...]

FACT FILE
GROUP: Carpet sharks	**EATS:** [...]
LENGTH: 8 ft (2.4 m)	**WEIG** [...]
LIVES: Indian Ocean & western Pacific	
DEPTH: 0–210 ft (0–65 m)	**HABITAT:** Coastal seabed
YOUNG: Lays egg cases	**FISHED:** Local

40 BLACK TIP REEF SHARK
Carcharhinus melanopterus

FIN TIPS
Black tips on tail and other fins

CAMOUFLAGE
Pale belly helps hide the shark against the light when viewed from below

FIELD NOTES
People wading off sandy beaches sometimes find this shark brushing against their legs as it frequently swims in water less than a few feet deep. It will even wriggle over sand flats with its black-tipped fins and back out of the water. Occasionally it will bite, confused by splashing feet.

FACT FILE
GROUP: Ground sharks	
LENGTH: 6 ft 6 in (2 m)	**EATS:** Fish, invertebrates
LIVES: Indian Ocean and southwest Pacific	**WEIGHT:** 30 lb (14 kg)
DEPTH: 3–250 ft (1–75 m)	**HABITAT:** Coral reefs
YOUNG: 2–4 live young	**FISHED:** Commercial

Profile Cards
Pull out these handy pocket-size cards and bone up on the essential facts that every expert should know. Use them to test your friends' knowledge, too. Or make some of your own cards to add to your collection!

Toxic spine, or "sting"

SHARK RELATIVES
Like sharks, skates and rays are cartilaginous fish. There are around 600 known species. All have wing[...] pectoral fins joined to the head and gill slits on the underside of a flattened body. Many skates and ray[...] spend their lives on or close to the seabed.

Barbel

SHARK SEN[...]
The pair of feelers, or b[...] on the nurse shark's nose[...] can sense prey such as s[...] in the sand. Many of th[...] on the seabed have ba[...] to probe [...]

DK EYEWITNESS WALL[CHARTS]

SHARK

MANY PEOPLE THINK of sharks as mean and menacing, with their pointed snouts, fearsome teeth, and staring eyes. Sharks are some of the largest and most successful of all marine predators, but only a few are a real danger to people. Sharks are one of three groups of cartilaginous fish, along with skates and rays, and a group of deepsea fish called chimeras. Most cartilaginous fish live in the sea, but a few sharks and some rays enter freshwater and certain tropical species live exclusively in freshwater.

Caudal fin

Gray to black upper body

Long gill slits

Triangular-shaped dorsal fin

HAMMER[...]

Mapping sharks

Mapping marine life in the oceans combines traditional skills of watching and recording with the latest computer technology. Distribution maps created from observations and tagging show where particular sharks are likely to be found, but maps for many species are still incomplete. Satellite data is analyzed by computers to make maps of the ocean currents used by sharks on their migrations.

Bird's-eye view

Small, low-flying, aircraft called microlights are ideal for spotting sharks that swim near the surface in clear ocean waters. The pilot can count the sharks, record their position, and guide researchers (or ecotour operators) who want to follow the sharks and tag them. Volunteers from conservation groups also help spot sharks from boats or clifftops, and some divers help to monitor shark populations.

Data tag attached to a shortfin mako

Shark tracking

Catching sharks, attaching tags, and releasing them has been used as a technique for tracking sharks for over 50 years. These simple tags are sent back when the animal is seen or caught again. Self-releasing pop-up satellite tags fixed to the shark's dorsal fin record water depth and temperature, as well as speed and position. Experts analyze all the data and use it to map what the shark has been doing as well as where it has been.

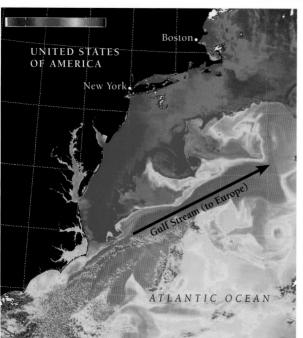

Going with the Gulf Stream

This map of ocean currents in the North Atlantic was generated by computers from data collected by the Terra satellite. Instruments on the satellite detect infrared radiation from the ocean which gives a measure of the water temperature. This in turn shows up important ocean currents which carry water of different temperatures from one place to another. The Gulf Stream, shown here in red, carries warm water from the Gulf of Mexico up the eastern coast of the US and then across the Atlantic toward Europe. It is this warm water that blue sharks and other species swim in during their migrations. Combining information on the direction, temperature, and speed of currents with tagging data helps scientists to work out the routes and timing of shark migrations.

Your *Eyewitness* map

The map in your pack shows how widely sharks are distributed over the globe. It marks the locations for 38 species about which most is known, as well as showing well-known pupping sites (where baby sharks, or pups, are born) and some of the main migration routes. Research institutes and fisheries compile databases on species that have been studied, sighted, photographed, filmed, captured, or tagged. Experts even learn to recognize individuals from their markings and scars. Gathering this information presents a challenge because sharks travel so much in the oceans and some species stay out in the open waters, out of sight.

Eyewitness
Shark
Map

Where sharks swim

Sᴀᴀʀᴋꜱ ᴀʀᴇ ꜰᴏᴜɴᴅ ɪɴ ᴏᴄᴇᴀɴꜱ ᴀʟʟ ᴏᴠᴇʀ ᴛʜᴇ ᴡᴏʀʟᴅ, although few venture into icy polar seas. Some species are spotted by humans more often than others, because they prefer to stay in shallow coastal waters, while others are open-ocean voyagers. Follow the routes of 38 different shark species, color-coded into eight major groups. (See pages 6–7 of your Profile Cards for key features.) The arrows show some of the long migration routes of great white, blue, and shortfin mako sharks as they head off in search of food, mates, or warmer waters. Close to the shores, many sharks use sheltered sites for nurseries and some intrepid bull sharks visit inland rivers.
Enjoy your shark-tracking voyage!

LONG-DISTANCE TRAVELS

The blue shark is a regular long-distance traveler through tropical and temperate oceans. Atlantic blue sharks ride the Gulf Stream current as it sweeps eastward from the Gulf of Mexico. After mating in the western North Atlantic, some pregnant females move east to pup off southern Europe, and then return in a clockwise direction.

WANDERING FOR WARMTH

Shortfin mako sharks live in warm and tem... oceans. Their migration patterns reflect the... that they prefer a water temperature of ab... 62–72° F (17–22° C). Studies in their feedi... grounds off the coast of North America sh... that they move northward from June to O... returning south again during the winter...

FEE...

NORTH
AMERICA

Multimedia

Get creative with your school projects or produce your own expert-looking files. Packed with 100 specialized images and facts about sharks, this clip-art CD will make your work look so professional you'll be dying to show it off.

Clip-art CD

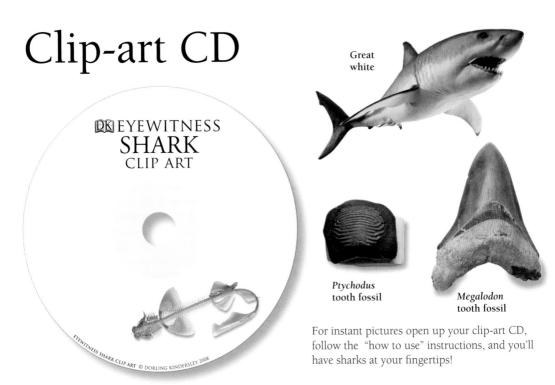

Great white

DK EYEWITNESS SHARK CLIP ART

EYEWITNESS SHARK CLIP ART © DORLING KINDERSLEY 2008

Ptychodus tooth fossil

Megalodon tooth fossil

For instant pictures open up your clip-art CD, follow the "how to use" instructions, and you'll have sharks at your fingertips!

Shark life cycles

Model shark

Build up your knowledge of a shark's anatomy by assembling your great white shark model. All of the pieces in your kit are shown here. You'll find step-by-step instructions on the following pages.

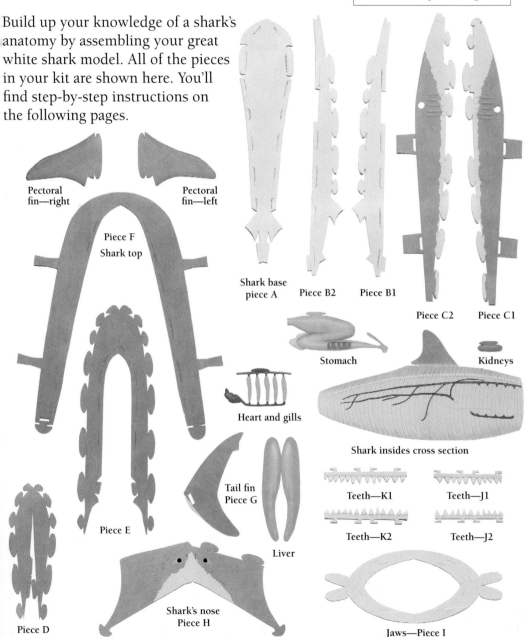

Pectoral fin—right

Pectoral fin—left

Piece F
Shark top

Shark base piece A

Piece B2

Piece B1

Piece C2

Piece C1

Stomach

Kidneys

Heart and gills

Shark insides cross section

Piece E

Tail fin Piece G

Teeth—K1

Teeth—J1

Teeth—K2

Teeth—J2

Piece D

Liver

Shark's nose Piece H

Jaws—Piece I

HELPFUL HINTS

Slotting the tabs together. When you select each piece of the model, first bend the sides of the tabs back along the score marks. For all of the shark pieces except the teeth, fold the sides of each tab together as you push the tab through the slot. Once the tab is in place, unfold the sides of the tab so that it lays flat once more. This will help each tab to stay firmly in place.

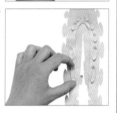

Shark base

Piece B1

Piece A

Slot in the tabs at the top first.

Piece B2

Remember fold back the tabs on the inside, once you have pushed them through.

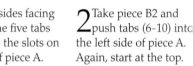

1 With white sides facing you, push the five tabs (1–5) of B1 into the slots on the right side of piece A.

2 Take piece B2 and push tabs (6–10) into the left side of piece A. Again, start at the top.

Piece A
Piece C1
Piece C2
Piece B1
Piece B2

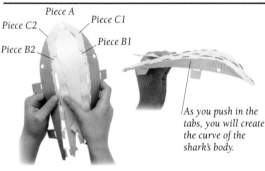

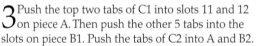

As you push in the tabs, you will create the curve of the shark's body.

Piece C2
Slot together here.
Piece C1

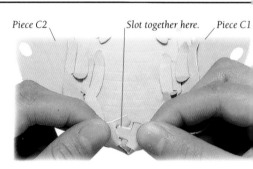

3 Push the top two tabs of C1 into slots 11 and 12 on piece A. Then push the other 5 tabs into the slots on piece B1. Push the tabs of C2 into A and B2.

4 Slot the nose-end tab of piece C1 (numbered 25) into the nose-end slot of piece C2. This secures the front bottom half of the shark's body.

Slot the tab on B2 behind the tab on B1 first.

B1 tab

Piece C1

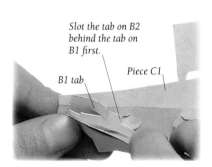

Pectoral fins
Large slot on C2 just below the gills.

Nose end

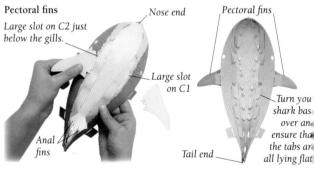

Anal fins

Large slot on C1

Tail end

Pectoral fins

Turn your shark base over and ensure that the tabs are all lying flat.

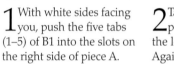

5 Making sure that the anal fins stay outside the body, slot the tab on piece B2 behind the tab on B1 at the tail end of the shark's body.

6 Slot the tab of the right pectoral fin into the large slot on the base of piece C1. Push the tab of the left pectoral fin through the slot on the other side—on C2. Set the completed bottom half of your shark aside while you make the nose.

Shark nose

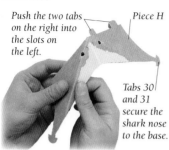

Push the two tabs on the right into the slots on the left.

Piece H

Tabs 30 and 31 secure the shark nose to the base.

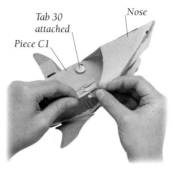

Tab 30 attached

Piece C1

Nose

Fold back the tabs.

7 Fold along the scored lines of the shark's nose to get the triangle nose shape. Slot the piece together at the top of the nose.

8 Attach the nose to the body by pushing tab 30 into the round slot on the front edge of piece C1. Do the same on the other side.

9 The tabs fold back inside the hole to secure the nose so that the jaw will open and shut!

Shark top

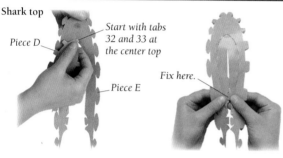

Piece D

Start with tabs 32 and 33 at the center top

Piece E

Fix here.

As you fix in the tabs, you will create a curve on the top side of the body.

Piece E

Piece F

Start with tabs 46 and 47 at the center top.

Turn your shark section over and make sure that tabs are opened out flat inside.

10 Take the center top piece D and, starting at the top, slot the tabs on both sides into piece E.

11 Fix the two sides of piece D together at the tail end by pushing tab 44 into the slot opposite.

12 Take piece F, and starting at the top in the center, push the 16 tabs of piece E through the slots on piece F. Continue round on both sides as before.

Shark tail

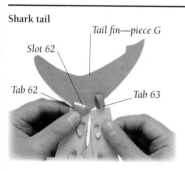

Tail fin—piece G

Slot 62

Tab 62

Tab 63

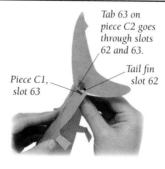

Tab 63 on piece C2 goes through slots 62 and 63.

Piece C1, slot 63

Tail fin slot 62

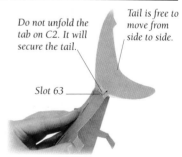

Do not unfold the tab on C2. It will secure the tail.

Tail is free to move from side to side.

Slot 63

13 Turn the shark model over so that the inside is facing you. Tuck tab 62 through the tail fin (slot 62) and hold the tab flat.

14 Now tuck tab 63 on C2 through the same tail fin slot, in the opposite direction, as shown above.

15 Bend tab 63 over and tuck it into slot 63 on piece C1. The end of the tab is hidden and the tail is secure.

Jaws and teeth

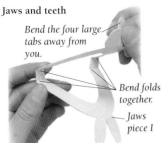

Bend the four large tabs away from you.

Bend folds together.

Jaws piece I

16 Bend the four scored folds on the jaws, piece I, toward you, to fold them in half. Then bend the four large tabs in the opposite direction.

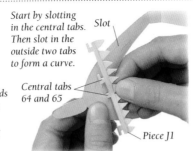

Start by slotting in the central tabs. Then slot in the outside two tabs to form a curve.

Slot

Central tabs 64 and 65

Piece J1

17 Slot teeth in rows inside the jaws. Put in the two rows of back teeth first (J1 and J2). Press the center L-shaped tabs in place first, then slot in the outer tabs.

Piece J2
Piece J1
Piece K1

18 Now slot in the two rows of front teeth (K1 and K2) Again start with the tabs in the center (72 and 73) and curve the teeth as you slot the tabs in place.

OPTIONAL GLUE
You can use a little craft glue to fix the jaws into the shark's nose. It is not essential—the teeth will stay in the model without glue.

Glue 4 x tabs

19 With the teeth facing toward you, dab a little glue on to the front of the four tabs of the jaws. Two at the top and two at the bottom.

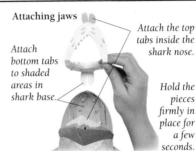

Attaching jaws

Attach the top tabs inside the shark nose.

Attach bottom tabs to shaded areas in shark base.

Hold the pieces firmly in place for a few seconds.

20 Firmly press the four large tabs at the bottom and top of the jaw to the corresponding shaded areas on the model, inside the shark base and nose.

You can also glue these in place with craft glue to strengthen the model, but it's not necessary.

21 Fold over the four main large tabs on the sides of the base of the shark you made earlier. Then do the same with the tabs on the top half of the shark.

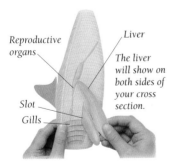

Reproductive organs

Liver

The liver will show on both sides of your cross section.

Slot
Gills

22 Push one side of the liver through the large slot on the cross-section piece just below the gills.

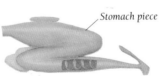

Stomach piece

23 With the digestion side of the cross section facing you, slot in the stomach.

Kidney piece

24 Turn the cross section over to the circulation side. Attach the kidney by pushing its tab into slot 89 above the liver.

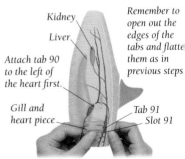

Kidney

Liver

Remember to open out the edges of the tabs and flatten them as in previous steps

Attach tab 90 to the left of the heart first.

Gill and heart piece

Tab 91
Slot 91

25 Attach the gill and heart piece to the blood circulation side of the cross section by slotting in tab 91.

INTERNAL ORGANS

A great white can take a long time to digest its meals. Digestion starts in the stomach and from there the food passes into the short intestine where it goes round and round inside a spiral valve. Digestive juices finish breaking it down and the nutrients are absorbed into the body. Waste leaves the body through the cloaca.

Liver

The liver of a great white can be 25 percent of its body weight. It contains a mix of oils that is lighter than seawater and helps keep the shark buoyant.

Circulatory system

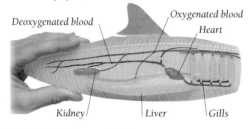

Deoxygenated blood
Oxygenated blood
Heart
Kidney
Liver
Gills

Digestive system

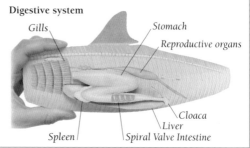

Gills
Stomach
Reproductive organs
Cloaca
Liver
Spleen
Spiral Valve Intestine

Large slot
Dorsal Fin

Completed model

Dorsal fin
Tail fin
Anal fin
Gill slits
Pectoral fin

The cross section of shark organs hangs inside the shark.

Moveable jaw

26 Take the cross section and push the dorsal fin through the large slot at the top of the shark so that the dorsal fin pops out of the top.

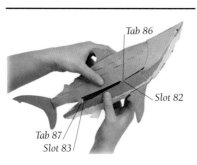

Tab 86
Slot 82
Tab 87
Slot 83

27 Carefully slot the two halves of the shark body together by pushing the tabs on the top into the slots opposite.

Index

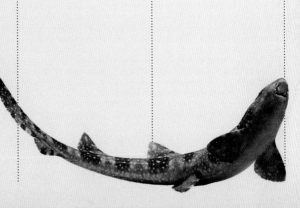

Activity answers

Pages 30–31 Which am I?
Shark
1. Cartilage skeleton
2. Oil-filled liver
3. Rigid fin
4. Sandpapery skin
5. No cover on gill slits
6. Mouth beneath snout

Bony fish
1. Gas-filled swim bladder
2. Scaly skin
3. Bony skeleton
4. Flexible fin
5. Covered gill slits
6. Mouth at end of snout

Bony fish or shark?
A. Shark
B. Bony fish
C. Bony fish
D. Shark
E. Shark
F. Bony fish
G. Shark

Pages 32–33 What do I eat?
1. Port Jackson shark
2. Tiger shark
3. Basking shark
4. Smooth hammerhead shark
5. Great white shark
6. Sand tiger shark

Shark snacks
A. Squid, 6
B. Turtle, 2
C. Mussels, 1
D. Plankton, 3
E. Seal, 5
F. Spotted ray, 4

Pages 34–35 Super senses
1. Hearing (ears)
2. Touch (barbels/feelers)
3. Electro-sense (ampullae of Lorenzini/ sensory pores)
4. Distant-touch (lateral line)
5. Sight (eye)
6. Smell (nostril)

Find the tail
1. C, Thresher shark
2. A, Great white shark
3. B, Swell shark
4. E, Tiger shark
5. D, Spotted ray

Pages 36–37 Who am I?
A. Common saw shark, 4 ft 6 in (1.4 m)
B. Frilled shark, 6 ft 6 in (2 m)
C. Goblin shark, 12 ft 10 in (3.9 m)
D. Zebra shark, 8 ft (2.4 m)
E. Thresher shark, 18 ft 8 in (5.7 m)
F. Great hammerhead shark, 20 ft (6.1 m)
G. Whale shark, 65 ft 6 in (20 m)
H. Pygmy shark, 11 in (28 cm)
I. Oceanic white tip shark, 13ft (4 m)
J. Shortfin mako, 13ft 2 in (4 m)

Pages 38–39 Where am I?
1. Arctic
2. Atlantic
3. Indian
4. Pacific
5. Southern

Compass
1. North
2. Northeast
3. East
4. Southeast
5. South
6. Southwest
7. West
8. Northwest

Place the shark
A. Velvet belly lantern shark, 2–4
B. Port Jackson, 4 and 3
C. Leopard, 4
D. Nurse, 2, 4
E. Basking, 1–4
F. Great white, 2–5
G. Blacktip reef, 3, 4
H. Bull, 3, 4, 2–4
I. Blue, 2–4

Acknowledgments

The publisher would like to thank the following for their kind permission to reproduce their photographs

(Key: a–above; b–below/bottom; c–center; f–far; l–left; r–right; t–top)

Expert Files
Alamy Images: Mary Evans Picture Library 22bl; Jeff Rotman 19b; **Ardea:** Valerie Taylor 21br, 24cl, 25br; **The Bridgeman Art Library:** Museo Archeologico Nazionale, Naples, Italy 25tl; **Dan Burton:** 20bl; **Corbis:** Tobias Bernhard/zefa/ 1; **Fabien Cousteau:** 21cr, 21tr; **Dr. Frances Dipper:** 29tr; **Getty Images:** Jan Sonnenmair/Aurora 23tr; Martin Barraud/Stone+ 2–3; Koichi Kamoshida 26–27; **Rachel Graham:** 8bl, 8tc, 8-9, 10l, 10tc, 11br, 11tc, 11tl, 12b, 12crb, 12tc, 12tl, 13c, 13tl, 13tr, 14b, 14cr, 15bc, 15tr, 19cr; **imagequestmarine.com:** Mark Conlin/V&W 54bl; **NASA:** Visible Earth http://visibleearth.nasa. gov/ Images courtesy Liam Gumley, MODIS Atmosphere Team, University of Wisconsin-Madison

Cooperative Institute for Meteorological Satellite Studies; 55tl; **naturepl.com:** Jeff Rotman 18b; **PA Photos:** AP/PA Photos 23c; **Photolibrary:** Pacific Stock 16b; Ed Robinson 6-7; **Simon Rogerson:** Dive Magazine www.divemagazine.co.uk 18tl; **The Ronald Grant Archive:** 22cr; Science Faction Images: Louie Psihoyos 40-41; **Science Photo Library:** F.S. Westmorland 17tr; **SeaPics.com:** C & M; Doug Perrine 24tr.

Map
Ardea: Douglas David Seifert ftr; **Geoff Beech:** cra; **Corbis:** Amos Nachoum ftl; **Photolibrary:** Richard Herrmann tl; Gerard Soury cla; **SeaPics.com:** C & M Fallows tr.

Profiles
See page 16 of *Shark Profiles*

Wall chart
See page 72 of *Eyewitness Shark*

Clip-art CD
See the *Credits* on the CD

All other images © Dorling Kindersley
For further information see: **www.dkimages.com**

The publisher would also like to thank:
Boundford.com for cartography on the Map;
Stewart Wild for proofreading;
Hilary Bird for the index;
Margaret Parrish for Americanization.